Aesop's Fables

Bob Chilcott

for SATB and piano

Composer's note

Aesop, supposedly a slave in Ancient Greece, lived sometime during the sixth century BC, but his wisdom is timeless, as is seen in these stories that are still enjoyed by both children and adults all over the world. I have used the translation made in the nineteenth century by the Reverend George Fyler Townsend, and have set only five out of more than six hundred that were supposedly written by Aesop. At the beginning of each story in my setting the title is spoken, as is the moral that comes at the end. I imagined these lines being spoken with great character, unpitched, and in the mood of the song. The final song in the set, 'The Goose and the Swan', is appropriately about singing. I have underpinned this song with a wonderful harmonic progression taken from 'Du bist die Ruh' by the king of all songwriters, Franz Schubert.

Duration: *c*.16 minutes

Contents

MUSIC DEPARTMENT

OXFORD

UNIVERSITY PRESS

OXFORD
UNIVERSITY PRESS

Great Clarendon Street, Oxford OX2 6DP, England
198 Madison Avenue, New York, NY 10016, USA

Oxford University Press is a department of the University of Oxford.
It furthers the University's aim of excellence in research, scholarship,
and education by publishing worldwide in

Oxford New York
Auckland Bangkok Buenos Aires Cape Town Chennai
Dar es Salaam Delhi Hong Kong Istanbul Karachi Kolkata
Kuala Lumpur Madrid Melbourne Mexico City Mumbai Nairobi
São Paulo Shanghai Taipei Tokyo Toronto

Oxford is a registered trade mark of Oxford University Press
in the UK and in certain other countries

ISBN 978-0-19-336179-9

Music and text origination by
Enigma Music Production Services, Amersham, Bucks.
Printed in Great Britain on acid-free paper by
Halstan & Co. Ltd., Amersham, Bucks.

for the Centenary Celebrations of Eltham Choral Society

Aesop's Fables

1. The Hare and the Tortoise

Aesop (6th cent. BC)
trans. by George Fyler Townsend (1814–1900)

BOB CHILCOTT

First performed on 29 March 2008 at Holy Trinity Church, Eltham, London, by Eltham Choral Society, conducted by Nicholas Jenkins, with Christopher Eastwood at the piano.

Printed in Great Britain

OXFORD UNIVERSITY PRESS, MUSIC DEPARTMENT, GREAT CLARENDON STREET, OXFORD OX2 6DP

-greed that the Fox should choose the course and fix the goal.

On the day ap-point-ed for the race the two start-ed to-

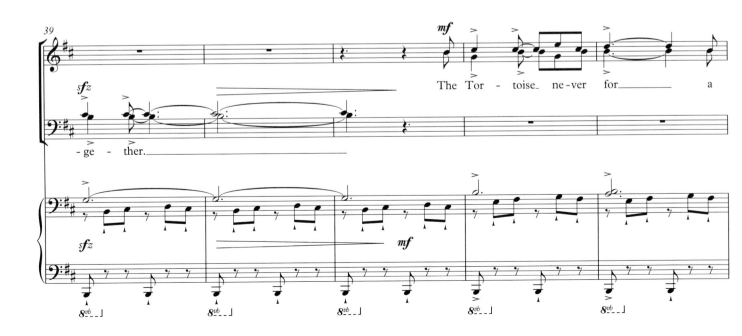

-ge - ther.

The Tor - toise ne-ver for a

mo - ment stopped, but went on with a slow but stea - dy

pace straight to the end of the course, the

course, the course.

2. The Mountain in Labour

Loud groans and noi - ses were heard, *ff* and

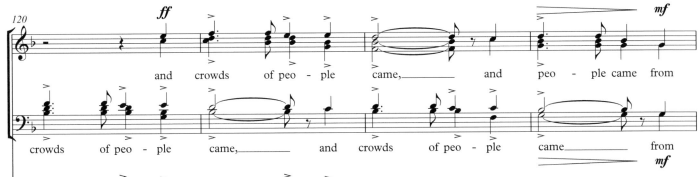

and crowds of peo - ple came, and peo - ple came from

crowds of peo - ple came, and crowds of peo - ple came from

all parts to see what was the mat - ter, the

out came a Mouse.

unis. (spoken)

T./B.

'Don't make much a - do,

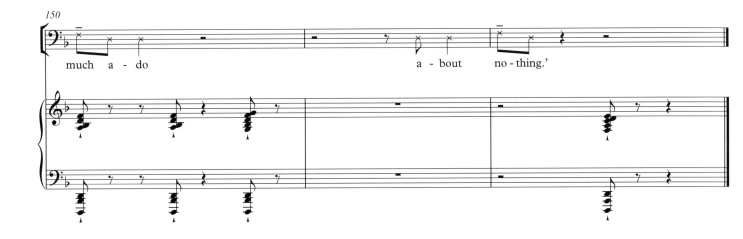

much a - do

a - bout no - thing.'

3. The Fox and the Grapes

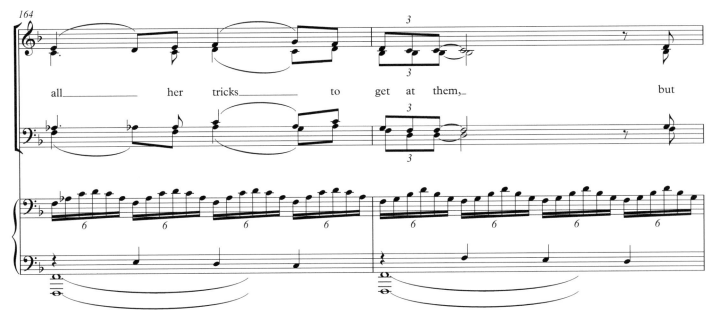

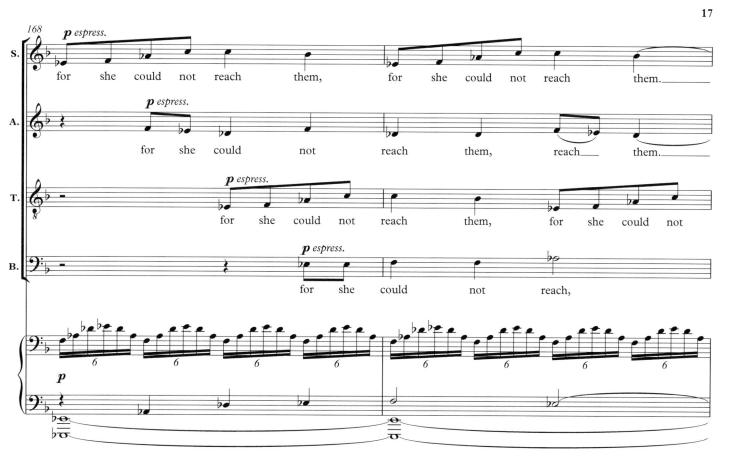

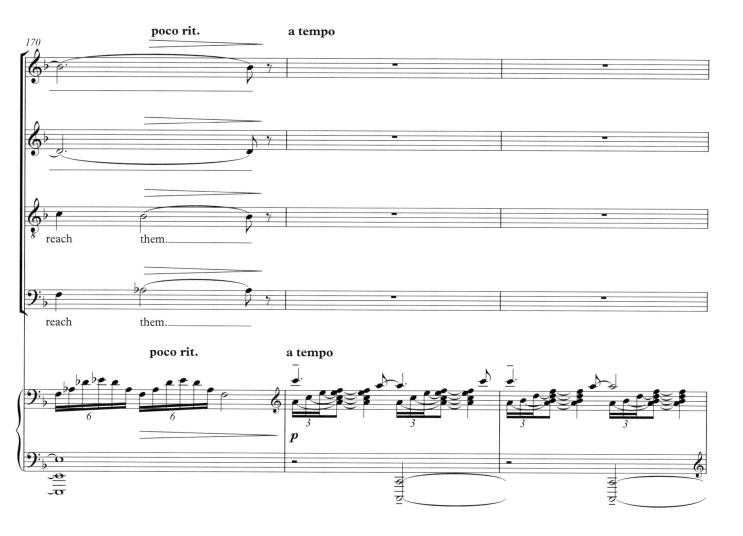

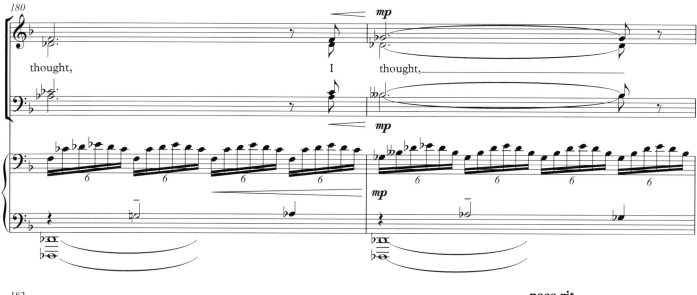

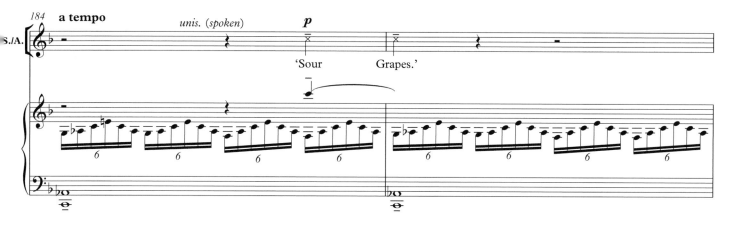

4. The North Wind and the Sun

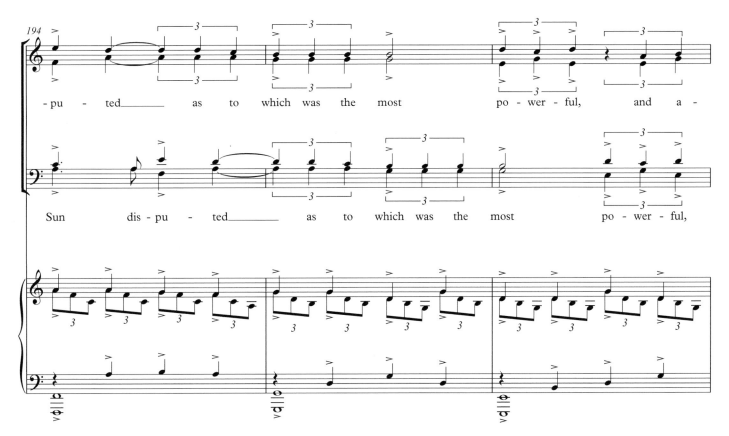

-pu – ted_____ as to which was the most po – wer – ful, and a –

Sun dis – pu – ted_____ as to which was the most po – wer – ful,

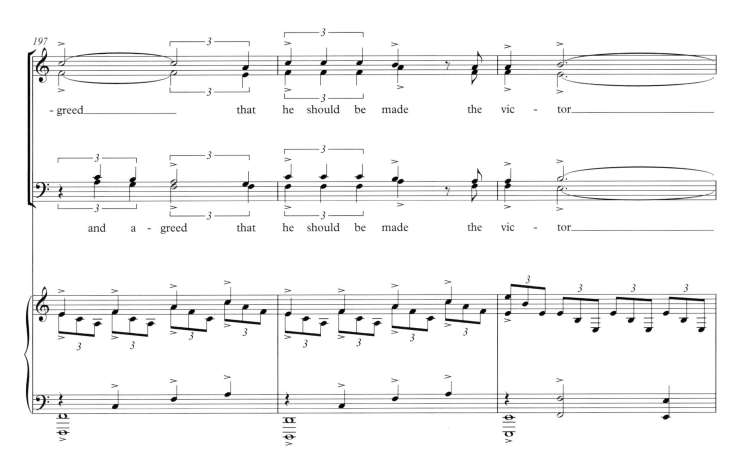

- greed_____ that he should be made the vic – tor_____

and a – greed that he should be made the vic – tor_____

who could first strip a way - far - ing man of his

clothes.

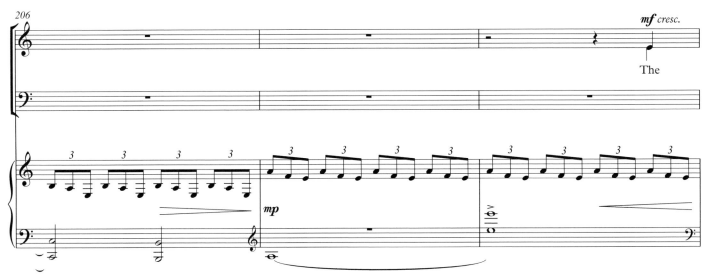

The

keen - er his blasts, _____ the clo - ser the Tra - vel - ler

keen - er his blasts, _____ the Tra - v'ller

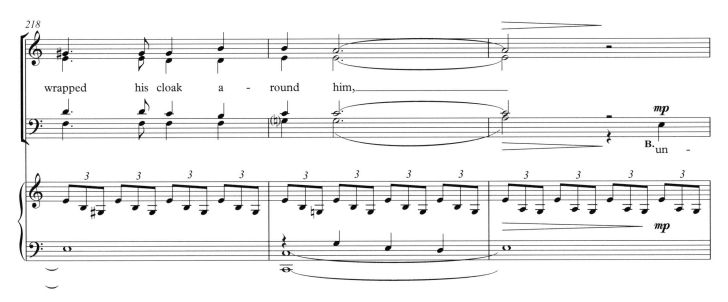

wrapped his cloak a - round him, _____

B. un -

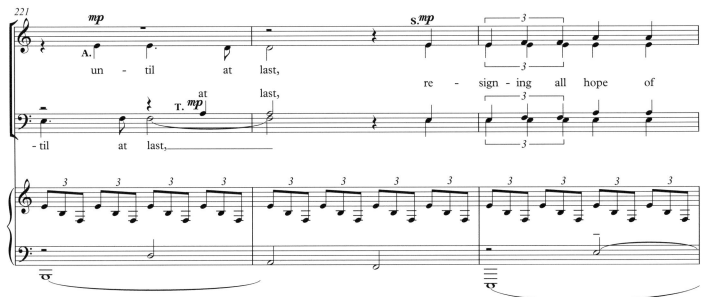

un - til at last, re - sign - ing all hope of

at last,

- til at last, _____

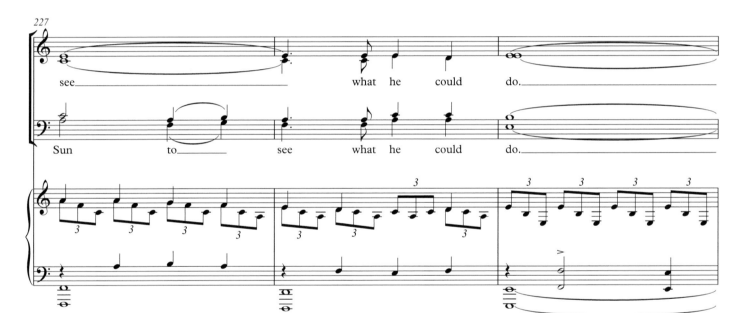

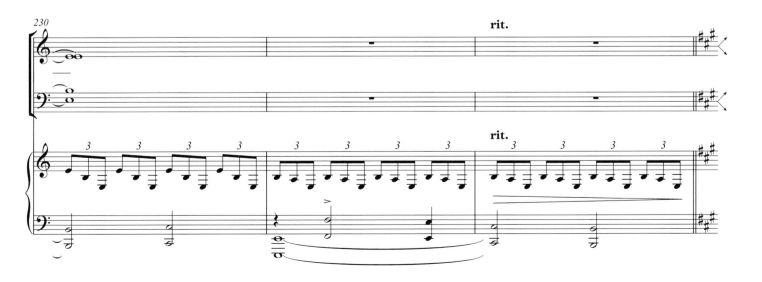

251

o - ver-come with heat, un - dressed and

heat, with heat, un - dressed and

heat, with heat, un - dressed and

- come with heat, un - dressed and

254

S.
A.

bathed in a stream that lay in his

T.
B.

mp

257

path.

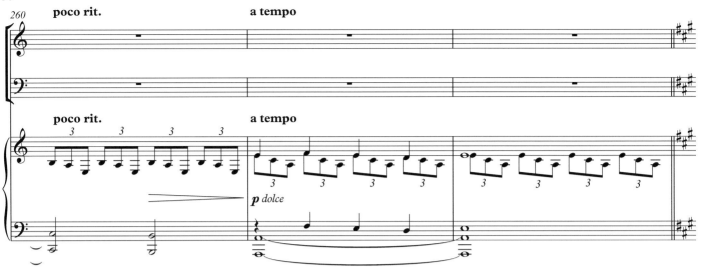

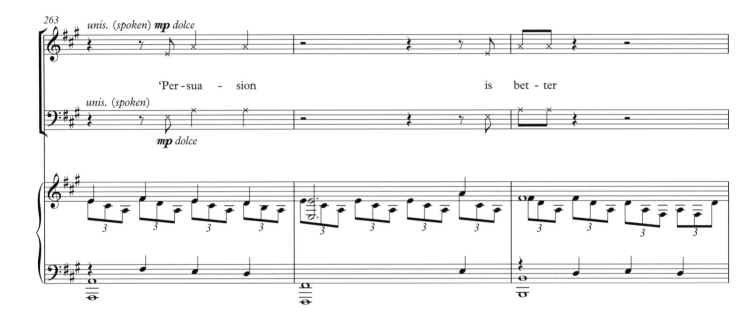

'Per - sua - sion   is   bet - ter

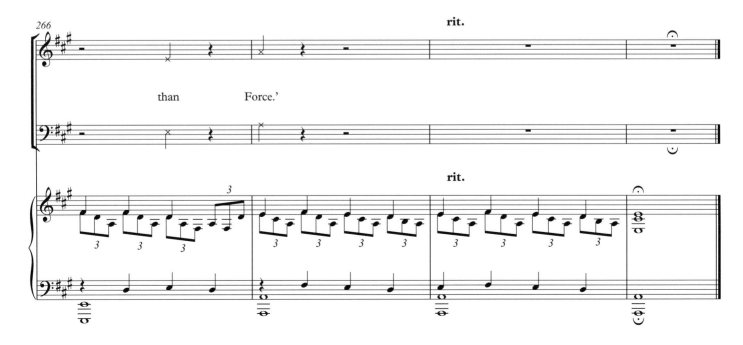

than   Force.'

5. The Goose and the Swan

mar - ket   a Goose and a Swan,_____   a Goose and a Swan._____

He fed   the   one for his ta - ble   and kept   the_   o - ther

for the sake of its song,_____   the sake   of its   song._____

When the time came for kill-ing the Goose, the cook went to get him at

night, when it was dark, and was not

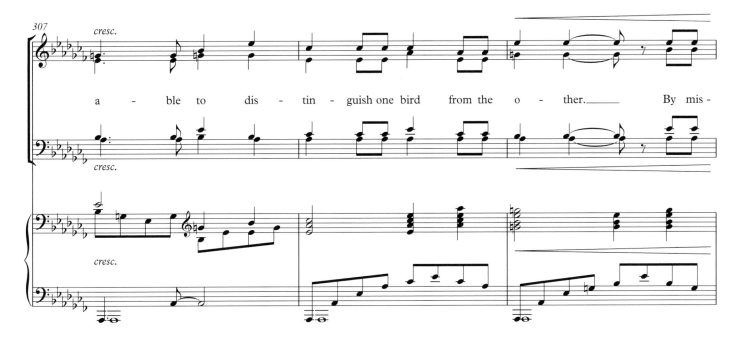

a - ble to dis - tin - guish one bird from the o - ther._____ By mis-

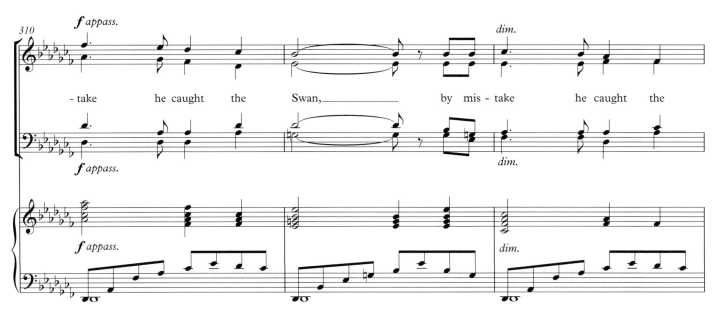

-take he caught the Swan,_____ by mis-take he caught the

Swan in-stead of the Goose._____

The Swan, threat-ened with death,____

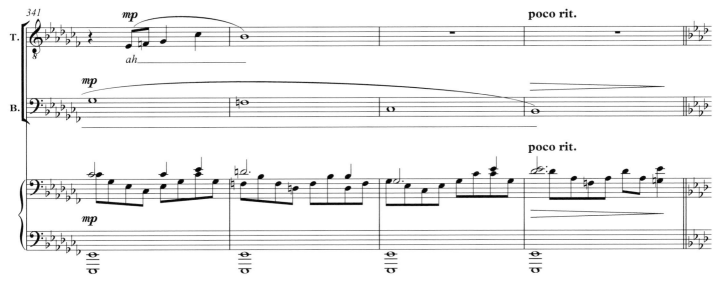

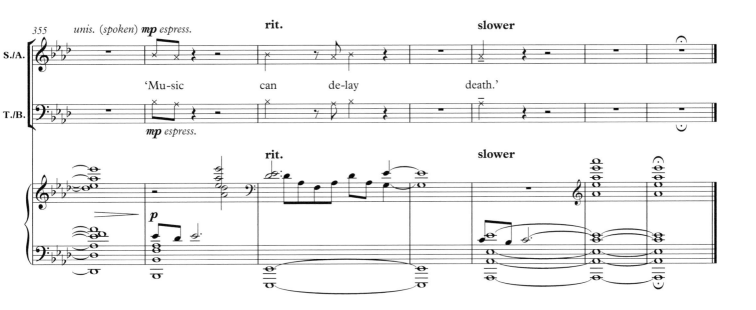

'Mu-sic can de-lay death.'